# MY PET GERBIL

## Carol Koopmans

WEIGL PUBLISHERS INC.
"Creating Inspired Learning"
www.weigl.com

Published by Weigl Publishers Inc.
350 5th Avenue, 59th Floor
New York, NY  10118
Web site: www.weigl.com

Project Coordinator
Heather C. Hudak

Design
Terry Paulhus

Library of Congress Cataloging-in-Publication Data available upon request.
Fax 1-866-44-WEIGL for the attention of the Publishing Records department.

ISBN 978-1-61690-073-1 (hard cover)
ISBN 978-1-61690-074-8 (soft cover)

Printed in the United States of America in North Mankato, Minnesota
1 2 3 4 5 6 7 8 9 0  14 13 12 11 10

052010
WEP264000

Photograph and Text Credits
Weigl acknowledges Getty Images as its primary image supplier for this title.

# Contents

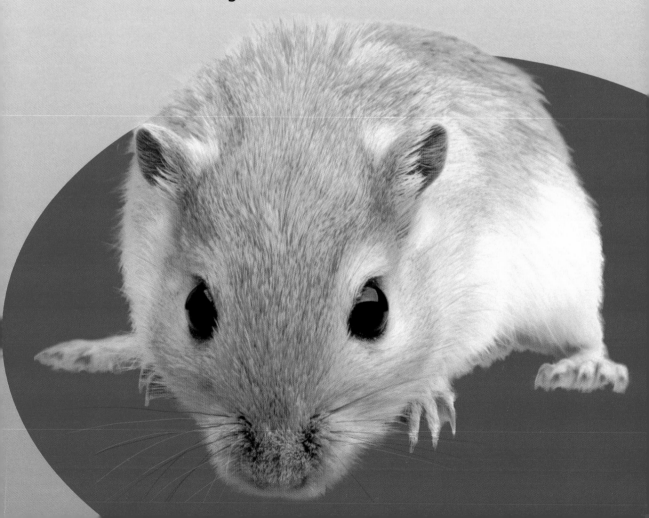

# Gentle Gerbils

Gerbils make excellent pets. They are small, clean, and inexpensive. They have a curious nature. Gerbils like playing, wrestling, climbing, and cuddling.

Healthy gerbils like to investigate new people and places.

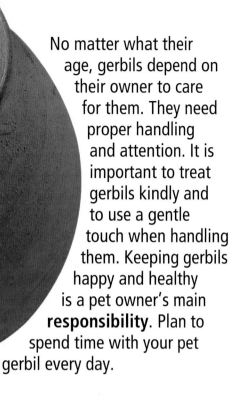

No matter what their age, gerbils depend on their owner to care for them. They need proper handling and attention. It is important to treat gerbils kindly and to use a gentle touch when handling them. Keeping gerbils happy and healthy is a pet owner's main **responsibility**. Plan to spend time with your pet gerbil every day.

The gerbil's tiny size, bright eyes, soft fur, twitching nose, and constant activity adds to his appeal. Watch your pet closely as he eats, sleeps, explores, and plays. You can have many hours of fun. The more you watch, the more you will learn about your gerbil.

# Playful Pets

- Do not be alarmed if gerbils stand on their hind legs and box at one another with their front paws. They are "play boxing."
- Playmates are important to gerbils. There should be at least two gerbils living together in one cage. If a gerbil does not have a playmate, he may become lonely and very quiet.
- Gerbils will spend hours exploring objects placed inside their cage.

# Pet Profiles

Gerbils are small **rodents**. They are plumper than mice and smaller than hamsters. There are 16 different **genuses** of gerbils. Within these genuses, there are more than 100 known **species**. More than 30 of these species are available as pets. They come in many different sizes, shapes, and colors. Some species of pet gerbils are also known as jirds. This is an Arabic word meaning "large desert rodent." Gerbils were named for the dry desert regions in India, Africa, Central Asia, and the Middle East, where they were first discovered. People can use the words "jirds" and "gerbils" to mean the same thing.

## mongolian

- Also known as the clawed jird
- Comes in many colors
- Social, even tempered
- Cautious until trust is gained
- Long hind legs for jumping
- Hardy and healthy
- Bonds to a mate or a friend for life
- Most common pet gerbil

## shaw's jird

- Darker fur and larger ears
- Males grow up to 14 inches (35.6 centimeters) long
- Large teeth that can cause damage
- Tail ends with a small furry tuft
- Very social; rarely bites
- Very smart, easy to train
- **Gnaws** constantly

# HAIRY-FOOTED

- A type of **pygmy** gerbil
- Also known as the snowshoe gerbil
- Thin, almost hairless tail
- Sandy-colored back with a white belly
- Long, thin hind legs
- Large, hairy feet
- Active at night
- Needs very little water in desert climates

# LESSER EGYPTIAN

- Very small in size
- Short ears
- Sandy-colored back with white belly
- White around the eyes and mouth
- Hairy tail with dark tip
- Tail is usually longer than the body
- Curious, friendly, and clever
- Enjoys burrowing in sand

# BUSHY-TAILED JIRD

- Long, thin head with big ears
- Orange and yellow fur on back, white belly
- Long, black and white whiskers
- Curious, friendly, and clever
- Enjoys climbing

# DUPRASI JIRD

- Also known as the fat-tailed gerbil
- Tail is bare, pink, and thick
- Soft, fluffy yellow fur with gray base
- Calm; rarely bites people or tries to escape
- Can be aggressive toward other gerbils
- Sleeps most of the time

# Gerbil History

Peter Simon Pallas, an explorer from Germany, saw wild gerbils in the 1760s while traveling through central Asia. In the 1860s, a French priest named Armand David discovered the Mongolian gerbil. He described it as a "jumping desert rat." This animal became known by the scientific name Meriones, which means "little clawed warrior."

Moving to a new home can be stressful for a gerbil. Allow him time to get used t his new surroundings before taking him out to play.

The most common gerbil is the Mongolian gerbil. It is also called the clawed jird. Mongolian gerbils were first raised in Japan in the 1930s. In 1954, they were sent from Japan to the United States to be used for research. Gerbils became popular as household pets in the early 1960s.

In nature, Mongolian gerbils live in hot desert climates. They live as family groups or clans. There can be as many as 20 gerbils in a clan. Each clan lives in underground tunnels called burrows. Burrows can be nearly 20 feet (6 meters) long, and they have special places for nesting and storing food. Clans that live together in these underground tunnel systems are called colonies.

# Cavy Crazy

- Gerbils know colony members by their smell. They **groom** each other by licking. Their **saliva** carries a special odor.

- Gerbils from the same **litter** likely will get along better than gerbils from different litters.

# Life Cycle

It is exciting to bring a cute, furry gerbil home. Your new pet will depend on you for food, shelter, and attention. Gerbils live for two to four years. Like all pets, your gerbil will need special care at each stage of her life.

## Newborn Gerbils

A baby gerbil is called a pup. There usually are four to six pups in a litter. Pups are blind, hairless, and tiny. They are about as long as the last joint on your little finger. When pups are born, their ears are closed. By one week of age, tufts of fur begin to grow on their body. Within 10 days, baby gerbils are covered with fur. For the first two weeks of life, it is best not to disturb the nest. The mother should be left with her babies so they can feed on her milk.

## Two to Three Weeks

By two weeks, gerbils become active and scamper about on wobbly legs. This is the time when gerbils begin to learn leg and paw movements for burrowing. By three weeks, the gerbil's eyes will open, and they will begin to explore. At this age, gerbils can eat some plants and grains. They will still drink their mother's milk, too. A few days later, the gerbil's ears begin to unfold, and the gerbil can hear sounds.

## Five to Six Weeks

At five weeks of age, gerbils have good eyesight, hearing, and strong hind legs. They scamper about, so their mother must watch them constantly. She carries her babies to the safety of their nest by the scruff of the neck. At six to eight weeks of age, gerbils are fully grown. They eat grains and plants and no longer drink their mother's milk.

## Mature Gerbils

Gerbils mature very quickly. They begin mating between eight weeks and three months of age. A female gerbil will have pups until she is about two years old. By three years of age, a gerbil is called a senior. Senior gerbils move more slowly. A young gerbil will show respect to a senior.

# Noisy Newborns

- Newborn gerbils can be very noisy for the first few days of life. They may squeak constantly in their nest. When one gerbil squeaks, the rest like to join in.

# Picking Your Pet

Before choosing a gerbil, there are many factors to consider. Finding out all you can about gerbils before buying one will help you make the best choice. The following questions and answers can help you choose your pet.

12

Gerbils are social animals. They do not like to be alone and are happiest with many playmates.

## Which Type of Gerbil Should I Choose?

The Mongolian gerbil is the most common breed of pet gerbil. Mongolian gerbils come in a variety of colors, and they are available in many pet stores. Since gerbils enjoy living in pairs or groups, you should decide if you have the space to house more than one.

## How Old Should the Gerbil Be?

Young gerbils should stay with their mother until they are at least four weeks old. Gerbils up to six weeks of age can live together even if they do not know each other. However, older gerbils must be introduced slowly. Learning to bond with a gerbil from another clan can be stressful and scary. Sometimes, gerbils will fight. If fighting occurs, they must be kept apart.

## How Should I Pick and Prepare for My New Gerbil?

Choose a reliable pet shop or store to buy your gerbil. Make sure the gerbil is healthy. Check that his eyes are bright and shiny. Is his fur soft and fluffy with no scabs? Is his nose free of sores? Does his tail end with a tuft of fur? Watch how the gerbil moves around. If he is hiding in a corner, he may be shy. If the gerbil runs in circles, he may be nervous. Darting about means the gerbil is active and curious. Before bringing a new gerbil home, you will need to prepare a safe living area. Be sure that other family pets, such as dogs or cats, are kept away from your new gerbil.

# Jumpy Gerbil

- Gerbils nap every two to three hours. If a gerbil's sleep is interrupted, he may become cranky. The gerbil may then nip at anyone who tries to hold him.
- Gerbils may become startled and hurt themselves if they jump out of your hand.

# Gerbil Gear

Gerbils do not take up much space, but they need the right kind of housing. Their home should have good **ventilation** and must be large enough for easy movement.

Cedar and pine shavings cannot be used for bedding. If eaten by a gerbil, these shavings can cause serious health problems.

Gerbils will chew just about anything. For that reason, a cage with wood or plastic bars is not suitable. A gerbil's sharp teeth will gnaw through these types of bars. If you choose a metal cage, make sure the gerbil cannot squeeze between the bars. Sometimes, gerbils will kick their bedding through the bars when they are burrowing. This makes a mess around the cage. An aquarium or **terrarium** that does not have any openings on the sides is a good choice. To make a larger shelter, use tunnels to join the cages together.

Whichever kind of housing you choose, place the shelter in a quiet area. Set it away from drafts and extreme heat or cold. Place the shelter out of reach of other household pets. For added safety, the shelter should have a lid that closes with a latch or lock. Make a play area inside the shelter. Include a small teeter-totter, mini gym, or climbing blocks. Provide a tiny house or **sisal** ball for nesting or sleeping. Pet supply stores sell many types of small toys suitable for gerbils.

# Furry Fun

- Wooden toys should be chemical free. The chemicals found in dyes may be poisonous and cause your pet to become ill.
- Gerbils can chew on a variety of sticks, uncolored cardboard, and twigs. Gerbils will nibble these items to shreds, making a soft fluff that they add to their nest.
- Most gerbils like to dig. Providing your pet with the space and materials to practice this hobby will keep him happy.

# Gerbil Grains

Gerbils are herbivores. They mainly eat plants and grains. However, gerbils sometimes eat insects, too. It is important to feed a pet gerbil a healthy mix of grains, including oatmeal.

Gerbils will store their food to eat later. They will hide it in their bedding.

Every day, a gerbil eats about 0.5 ounces (14 grams) of food. Gerbils like to have a routine. Fill your gerbil's feeding dish at the same time each day. Fruits provide some moisture for gerbils. However, fresh fruits are sweet, so they should only be fed to gerbils occasionally as treats.

Water should be made available at all times. A gerbil will drink about 0.25 ounces (7 g) of water each day. Hang a drip-free water dispenser from the side of the cage. Change the water daily so it is always fresh.

# Gerbil Grub

- Gerbils can hold seeds in their paws. They use their front teeth to peel the hull, spit it out, and enjoy the tasty **kernel**.
- Offer a gerbil a mealworm, a hard boiled egg, or some yogurt as a special treat. Pumpkin seeds and peanuts contain fat, so gerbils can only eat them rarely.
- Apples are safe for gerbils to eat, but too many can cause an upset stomach.
- Gerbils prefer fatty foods. Wait until they have eaten everything in their feed mix before refilling the bowl. This will ensure they have a healthy diet.

# Built for Burrows

From a small Mongolian gerbil to a larger Shaw's jird, all gerbils have similarities, such as large front teeth. Their features are suited to their way of life in nature.

# 7 Essential Parts of the Gerbil

Gerbils have small ears on the outside of their head. Their middle and inner ears are very large. This gives them excellent hearing. Baby gerbils can make a sound that only their mothers can hear.

Gerbils have powerful hind legs that are slightly longer than a hamster's legs. Gerbils use their legs for kicking and jumping. They kick dirt out of the way when they burrow.

Gerbils have dark eyes on the sides of their head. This allows them to spot danger in all directions.

Whiskers allow gerbils to feel their way around and sense nearby objects.

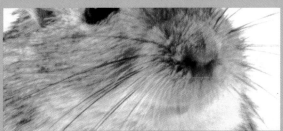

Gerbils have a small mouth, with teeth that never stop growing. Constant gnawing keeps their teeth short. If a tooth breaks, it grows back within two to three weeks.

Gerbils use their sense of smell to find food and locate other gerbils.

A gerbil's strong hind feet have five toes each. The front paws have four clawed toes each. The front paws are used for gripping, holding, and grooming.

# Gerbil Housecleaning

Gerbils like to have soft, clean bedding. Shredded paper, aspen wood chips, or processed corn cobs are good choices. Bedding should be packed at least 6 inches (15 cm) deep on the floor of the cage. Bedding this deep allows gerbils to burrow or make nests.

Gerbils keep their living areas in good order. They choose certain spots for sleeping, hiding, or storing food.

It is important to keep your gerbil's home tidy. Gerbils use one corner of their cage as a bathroom. The droppings should be removed from this area every day. A gerbil's food dish and water bottle should also be cleaned every day. Gerbils need clean bedding every week, too.

Your gerbil's entire cage will need to be cleaned every month, so it does not become dirty or begin to smell. You can wear rubber gloves to remove the bedding and bits of old food. Then, wash the cage floor with soap, water, and a bit of **disinfectant**. Be sure to rinse the cage well and allow it to dry before putting fresh bedding inside.

# Keeping Clean

- A sponge can be used to clean a gerbil's cage.
- Gerbils lick each other's fur to keep it clean and soft. They do not need to be bathed by their owner.
- Gerbils enjoy taking "sand baths." Fill a shallow dish with sand for this purpose.
- Your gerbil's food dish should be shallow with a flat bottom. It must be heavy enough to prevent tipping.

# Healthy and Happy

Taking good care of a pet gerbil will help keep her healthy and happy. However, sometimes a pet gerbil can become ill. Signs of illness include drooling, constant scratching, and a poor appetite. Uneven breathing, matted fur, or a hunched back can also mean that the gerbil is sick. If your gerbil becomes very ill, he may need to visit a **veterinarian**.

A gerbil's cage should contain items that are similar to her natural habitat.

Gerbils like to explore outside their cage every day. Your gerbil may enjoy playing with an exercise ball. This is a plastic ball that has an opening for the gerbil to crawl inside. The enclosed ball is a safe place for a gerbil to play. She can run around inside the ball, causing it to roll.

Young pups can be injured on ladders or exercise wheels. These items can be added to your gerbil's cage when she is at least six weeks old. When buying an exercise wheel to attach to the side of the gerbil's cage, consider a type with solid spokes. A wheel with open spokes is not a good choice. The gerbil's tail or legs can become caught in the spokes.

Some gerbils can become ill in stressful situations. They do not enjoy loud noises or being handled often. Set up the gerbil's cage in a quiet place in your home. Gerbils are always aware when danger is near. Other household pets, such as cats, dogs, birds, or snakes, can be a threat to your gerbil. These animals should be kept far away from the gerbil's living area. This will help the gerbil feel safe.

# Staying Safe

- When gerbils sense danger or become nervous, they produce a loud thumping noise. This noise is made by pounding both of their back feet on the floor at the same time.
- Gerbils may become ill if they are too cold or too hot.

- Gerbils have a gland on their stomach that produces a strong-smelling oil. Gerbils mark their territory by rubbing their stomach against objects around them.

# Gerbil Behavior

Once your gerbil has safely settled into his new home, introduce yourself by putting your hand inside the cage. You can let him sniff your hand. Hold a treat in your fingers. Once you have gained the gerbil's trust, he will begin eating the treats from your fingertips. Over time, he will climb into your hand and eat. Then, you can begin holding him.

Hold your gerbil over soft bedding or near a flat surface so he will not be hurt if he slips from your hands.

If you swoop your hand inside the cage to pick up the gerbil, he may mistake you for a bird. In nature, birds hunt gerbils. The swooping action may frighten the gerbil, and he might try to hide. You may lose the gerbil's trust. It is important to learn the proper way to handle a pet gerbil so that he feels safe.

To pick up a gerbil correctly, cup the palms of your hands, and use them like a scoop. A sense of nestling in your safe hands may keep the gerbil from jumping or escaping. In order to gain your gerbil's trust, handle him often. Over time, he will become familiar with your touch and your scent.

## Pet Peeves

**Gerbils do not like:**
- being handled roughly, held tightly, or squeezed
- sudden loud noises or unexpected movements
- poor quality food with little variety
- being picked up by their tail

# Rodent Relationship

- If you are wearing a shirt with a pocket, your gerbil may try to nestle in it. This has earned them the nickname "pocket pets."
- Grooming each other is a way that gerbils bond with one another.
- It will take time to earn your gerbil's trust.

# Judging Gerbils

Owning a gerbil can provide hours of fun. Many pet owners are proud of their gerbils. They enjoy showing their frisky little friends at pet shows. Attending a gerbil show will give you the chance to ask questions of people who know a great deal about gerbils. It is a fun way to get information. By meeting other gerbil owners, you can share gerbil stories. Displays at these shows can give you many helpful tips about caring for your pet, too.

You can find out about gerbil shows in your community and around the country by contacting a local gerbil club.

## Gerbil Trouble

In David A. Adler's *The Many Troubles of Andy Russell*, a boy named Andy has seven pet gerbils that have escaped from their cage and are running around the basement. Andy is running late for school again, and he does not want to give his Grade 4 teacher a reason to report his behavior to his parents. To top it all off, Andy's friend Tamika needs his help. Tamika's family is moving. Andy wants to ask his parents if Tamika can move in with them. Andy runs into one setback after another as he tries to collect his gerbils and make everything right again. If you enjoy *The Many Troubles of Andy Russell*, you can read more about Andy's adventures in other books in David A. Adler's Andy Russell series.

Entering your pet in a gerbil show allows him to be judged for his special features, such as the quality of his fur. Before you enter the show, learn the standards judges use for determining a gerbil's special features.

To enter a gerbil show, owners are required to register their pet by filling out a special form. Often, there is a small entry fee to show a gerbil. Pet shows are held in many places throughout the year. Begin by checking with your local pet club. There may be a list of dates and locations for shows. Pet clubs also offer facts about gerbils. This may include information about housing, breeding, diseases, and gerbil standards.

# fun facts

- Gerbils stand on their hind legs to look around or to test their jumping skill.
- Wearing strong perfumes or spraying air freshener near a gerbil's cage can confuse him. Gerbils learn to recognize their owner's natural scent. If the scent is masked by perfume, the gerbil may not recognize his owner.

# Pet Puzzlers

What have you learned about gerbils? If you can answer the following questions correctly, you may be ready to own a pet gerbil.

**Q** Should I give my pet gerbil a bath?

**A** Gerbils are very clean. They lick themselves and other gerbils. Licking helps to keep the fur smooth and clean. There is no need to bathe a gerbil!

**Q** How many years do gerbils usually live?

**A** Gerbils live two to four years.

**Q** What should I feed a pet gerbil?

**A** Gerbils mainly eat plants and grains. Sometimes, they eat insects. Gerbils enjoy vegetables, such as alfalfa sprouts, broccoli, carrots, peas, and celery.

**Q** What is another name for the Mongolian gerbil?

**A** The Mongolian gerbil is also known as the clawed jird.

**Q** Why are gerbils sometimes called "pocket pets"?

**A** Gerbils are called pocket pets because they sometimes enjoy hiding in shirt pockets.

**Q** How do gerbils use their strong hind legs?

**A** Gerbils use their hind legs for jumping and for making a thumping sound when they sense danger or are nervous.

**Q** What are a gerbil's front paws used for?

**A** A gerbil's front paws are used for gripping, holding, and grooming.

# Calling Your Gerbil

Before you buy your pet gerbil, write down some gerbil names that you like. Some names may work better for a female gerbil. Others may suit a male gerbil. Here are a few suggestions.

Whiskers

Silver

Sandy

Happy

Nosy

Fluffy

Taffy

Goldy

Rocket

# Frequently Asked Questions

## How can I keep my gerbil from escaping his cage?

Gerbils are curious. They will always be looking for an escape. The top of their enclosure should be locked so they cannot jump up and push off the lid. Provide gerbils with plenty of food, toys, and exercise equipment so they do not become bored.

## Does my gerbil need water if she eats vegetables often?

In nature, gerbils can survive without water if they eat plenty of vegetables. However, pet gerbils still need fresh water daily. Without water, pet gerbils will not live as long, their coat will not be healthy, and their body will be thinner.

## Is it safe for my gerbil to run around my room?

Gerbils need to run. They must have time every day to explore outside their cage. First, you must "gerbil-proof" the area where your pet will roam free. To do this, you must block all escape paths. Put up barriers that gerbils cannot jump over, run under, or scoot around. Unplug and remove all electrical cords. Keep all other household pets in another part of the house.

# More Information

## Animal Organizations

You can help gerbils stay healthy and happy by learning more about them. Many organizations are dedicated to teaching people how to care for and protect their pet pals. For more gerbil information, write to the following organizations.

### American Gerbil Society

The American Gerbil Society, Inc.
18893 Lawrence 2100
Mount Vernon, MO 65712

### Humane Society of the United States

2100 L Street N.W.
Washington, DC 20037

# Websites

For answers to your gerbil questions, visit the following websites.

### The American Gerbil Society

www.agsgerbils.org

### Pet Web Site

www.petwebsite.com/gerbils.asp

### Twin Squeaks Gerbils

www.twinsqueaks.com

# Words to Know

**disinfectant:** a chemical cleaner used to kill germs

**genuses:** a group of different, but related, plants and animals

**gnaws:** chews

**groom:** clean

**kernel:** the soft part inside the shell of a seed or nut

**litter:** a group of baby animals born at one time

**pygmy:** miniature in size

**responsibility:** to make good choices while performing a duty

**rodents:** mammals with large front teeth, which are used for gnawing

**saliva:** a colorless, tasteless liquid that is made by glands inside the mouth

**sisal:** stiff fiber used to make rope

**species:** a group of related animals

**terrarium:** a glass tank with a screen lid

**ventilation:** constant fresh air

**veterinarian:** animal doctor

# Index